ASHFORD
SCENES OF THE SIXTIES

STEVE R. SALTER

For Mum, Dad and James

For Richard Filmer

Dedicated to:

Vilma Rosaria Gizzi
1928–2018

David Robert Easton
1937–2019

First Edition 2019

ISBN 978-1-9996470-6-3

British Library Cataloguing-in-Publication Data
A catalogue record for this book is available from the British Library.

Published by Destinworld Publishing Ltd.
www.destinworld.com

CONTENTS

The heart of Ashford, May 1964.

INTRODUCTION

Time has certainly not stood still for the market town of Ashford, and with ongoing changes to its appearance and infrastructure, some would barely recognise the town that they once knew well. As a historian with a passion for preserving the heritage that surrounds us, it may be a bit alien for me to encourage modernity. To a degree, every town or city must move with the times and further develop itself but, that said, it certainly doesn't mean to say that I agree with all of it in Ashford's case. There have been scores of changes to our once-thriving market town over the decades, and almost all of them have been controversial to some degree.

Today, the rate and extent of change is a bitter pill to swallow for those of us old enough to remember how lifelong Ashfordians (and indeed newcomers) felt justifiable pride in their town. They not only loved the place, but also derived benefit from living here. Many of these changes have seen the town centre evolve, but certainly not for the better in a number of respects.

An ongoing process in recent years (not helped by those who set the business rates) has seen those once-familiar independent businesses and chains depart the town either through restructure or liquidation, leaving Ashford with gaping holes in its once-bustling shopping streets. Previously, there was little need to go elsewhere when it came to either buying everyday essentials or more specialist items, but now, unless you have a car, are familiar with public transport (or indeed can tolerate it), or have the internet, more and more we struggle to get what we want.

With M&S turning its back on the town centre and Debenhams set to follow suit early in 2020, Ashford will no longer have a department store to its name for the first time in well over a century. Alarmingly, those in power and tasked with making the town a desirable place to visit – and indeed live – seemingly appear untroubled by the state of play in the town centre, with consistent rumours that it is the authorities' long-term plan to turn the ailing High Street into a residential area. It is also rumoured that areas such as Elwick Road and the McArthur Glen Outlet represent the authorities' future vision for shopping in the town, and are said to be the prime choice of a 'new' High Street.

One sincerely hopes that new developments such as the Curious Brewery in Victoria Road and the boutique-style Picturehouse Cinema in Elwick Road on the original site of Ashford Market will establish firm and successful roots for sustainable business, though in the case of the latter, some Ashfordians questioned whether the town needed another cinema. At the time of writing, despite assurances from top authoritarians in the town, none of the units within the Elwick Place development set aside for restaurants and shops have been let for occupation. Despite it not being on the list of 'what residents want' (which has always been the case), Ashfordians wouldn't want the development to become a white elephant.

When looking back at the town in earlier eras, the first thing that shouts out to you is how the place *worked* and how *busy* it was. When comparing Ashford now to a street scene from, for example, the 1960s, it is nothing like it used to be. Looking at neighbouring towns and how they have ridden out the storm, one must question the motives and competence of the authorities in our town. Ashford is in many respects a place that is run by those who do not originate from the area, and thus perhaps do not always appreciate the views of those who know the town well.

Ashford – Scenes of the Sixties follows on from my hugely popular book *Ashford – Visual Recollections* and other titles, and provides those passionate about Old Ashford a unique and unrivalled glimpse of the town in the 'swinging sixties' through a portfolio of previously unseen images. Many of these rare photographs really give a feel for the town in an extremely different and to some extent now somewhat forgotten period. Indeed, it even serves to illustrate some of the poor planning practices endured back then – and the 'calm' before the significant and progressive destruction that has taken place. This new book is guaranteed to revive memories of the town from a gentler and more pleasant time.

Steve R. Salter
September 2019

CHAPTER 1

A TOWN TO TREASURE

Upper High Street, 1969. In the days before planners ruled and enforced, the town of Ashford was something of a gem in respect of how unspoilt it was. With its prominent array of independent traders and few chain stores, locals felt that they had everything they wanted in their town. Traffic still used the town centre, as this splendid image illustrates, with many saying today that pedestrianisation killed the passing-trade element. This view looks towards the one-time Castle Hotel with Lewis and Hyland's menswear department in the taller building (left), now demolished, with many long-lost trading names of the past such as International Stores and F.W. Woolworth. Today, a performance area is a key feature of this formerly bustling street which became pedestrianised in 1976. (Steve Salter Archive)

Upper High Street, 1969. The double-decker East Kent bus has moved away in this view taken further to the right depicting a busy shopping day. It's quite a novelty to see traffic lights within the heart of the town's streets nowadays, as in the High Street, for instance, they have been absent for some years. Hepworth's Tailors (pictured left) were in the town for many years at no. 83. The once-familiar chain was taken over by Next and the illustrated store premises became a travel agent for Lunn Poly (now TUI). Those central buildings stretching along New Rents (approximately above the red Ford Anglia) were demolished in 1972 for the Tufton Shopping Centre phases 1 and 2. (Steve Salter Archive)

Upper High Street, 1969. A fantastic view showing the heart of the High Street where it joins Kings Parade and Bank Street. You really do get the feel for 1960s Ashford from this pre-Ringway view that illustrates both defunct and departed chains that no longer have a presence in the town. After 84 years in the town at nos 74–76, Burton Menswear (previously Montague Burton) departed Ashford in 2016. Further along (centre) in May 2019, Marks & Spencer closed its store at County Square (which opened in 1978) after having previously traded on the High Street since 1934. Timothy Whites (centre) were consumed by Boots the Chemist in the 1980s and Granada Retail (right) within the former council chambers at Kings Parade, was a chain that disappeared from the town in the 1990s. Boots itself can be seen further down the High Street (centre right) at nos 60–62. (Steve Salter Archive)

Upper High Street junction with New Rents and Castle Street, September 1963. In the years prior to the major alterations in the town, several street surveys were undertaken with the probability that the locality in this image was subject of the redevelopment plans and earmarked for demolition. Once such area was the south side of the Upper High Street and New Rents. This view illustrates no. 107, F. Guttridge chemist just creeping into view on the left, with Brickies of Kent Ltd butcher (left) at no. 109 and Frank Palmer gentlemen's outfitter at nos 111–113. None of these businesses or the properties in which they traded from are in existence today. In 2019, Gamestation trades from the spot where these properties once stood. (Bryan Sales)

Upper High Street, September 1963. A nostalgic view illustrating the handsome premises of F. Guttridge Ltd, chemist, at no. 107 High Street. Many ladies of this era taking pride in their appearance will remember Parisien hairdressers on the upper floor above the chemist's. The aforementioned butchers Brickies of Kent can be seen on the right, with Frank Price 'man's shop' pictured (left) at no. 105, in the former premises of Court Bros furnishers. (Bryan Sales)

Upper High Street, September 1963.
Following the closure of Frank Price (pictured) and until the demolition of these properties for the Tufton Shopping Centre, one-time menswear chain Foster Bros occupied no. 105. The recently closed Marks & Spencer store now occupies this site. (Bryan Sales)

Upper High Street, September 1963.
Generations of local cyclists of yesteryear will remember the L. Burch cycle agents and electrical goods at no. 103, opposite the premises of James and Kither at no. 104 (which can be seen in the reflection of the shop window). The Burch family lived at no. 2 Park Road in the town for several years. (Bryan Sales)

Upper High Street, September 1963. Many items of jewellery, including wedding rings and watches, would have been purchased from jeweller J. Price (Ashford) Ltd when they traded in the town. When their premises pictured here at no. 101 were demolished, a generation of the Price family continued watch repairs in a much smaller unit within the Tufton Shopping Centre until the late 1980s. (Bryan Sales)

Upper High Street, September 1963. The beautiful ornate clock which once adorned the exterior of W.H. Gibbs furnishers premises at nos 97–99 High Street was reputed to have sat in a salvage yard for years following the demolition of these admirable premises together with their exquisite showrooms. The clock was restored in the late 1980s and moved to the exterior of NatWest Bank at no. 20 High Street. The reputable firm of Gibbs, whose owner was a local councillor in the town, relocated to North Street following the demolition of the illustrated premises, and operated from there until they ceased trading in the late 1970s. The High Street premises was well known for its regular furnishing exhibitions, with one advertised within the doorway for G-Plan furniture. (Bryan Sales)

Upper High Street, September 1963. Many housewives of the time will recall the existence of Eastman butcher at no. 95a which housed the typewriter repair works of Geerings behind the butchery premises. Eastmans were latterly bought by the long-lost Dewhurst chain which itself ceased trading in the early 2000s. Note the pram, complete with baby outside the neighbouring premises. How times have changed! One wouldn't dream of doing such a thing today. (Bryan Sales)

Upper High Street, September 1963. A wonderful view showing the one-time premises and business of R. & L. Hogg, grocers, at no. 95 High Street advertising Twinings tea, Bovril, Marmite and Birds Eye foods. The alleyway leading to the typewriter works can be seen on the left. (Bryan Sales)

Upper High Street, September 1963. The smart window displays and frontage of the menswear shop of Lewis and Hyland at no. 93 High Street, whose main department store stretched along New Rents. The entrance to the Ashtower Warehouse Company, another long-lost business (pictured left). Upon the redevelopment of this site, Lewis and Hyland took two linked and prime stores within the shopping centre, but had disappeared by 1980. (Bryan Sales)

Upper High Street, October 1963. One wonders how the town would have coped during the works to renew the main sewer (illustrated) from the upper to lower High Street. There was no ringway at the time and the street was still a significant route between the coast and London, even though the Ashford bypass existed for some of the route. It's immediately clear that this images dates from long before the Health and Safety at Work Act of 1974, as there are no hardhats in sight. (Bryan Sales)

13

Upper High Street junction with Castle Street, October 1963. Not so much of a worry for regulars at Crameri's restaurant (right) at nos 108–110 during its daytime trading hours, but one would hope that the makeshift safety railings would be adequate for those rolling out of the Castle Hotel at closing time. That's a sizable hole to fall into after a few beers! (Bryan Sales)

Upper High Street, October 1963. Further along the street, workmen prepare to lower the new modern concrete sewage pipes, replacing the antiquated brick-built sewers that were in dire need of replacement. Judging by the array of wares on display at Marcus Army and Navy stores, it can be presumed that the desert jackets were extra dusty with all that sand around! The Co-operative Chemist at no. 102 (centre left) latterly moved to Bank Street, and their premises were to become the Carpet Centre and then Matthews Butchers in the early 1980s. (Bryan Sales)

Upper High Street, October 1963. Among the works to replace the sewer, nostalgia sets in once more in this view which illustrates the much-loved and-missed James and Kither milliners and drapers at no. 104 and Knowles house furnishers at no. 106. Knowles disappeared from the town in the early 1980s, as did James and Kither – the latter being remembered for the old-fashioned money chutes that would run along the ceiling to the cashier. (Bryan Sales)

Upper High Street, 1964. A wonderful view showing the Upper High Street post-sewer replacement, demonstrating the influx of traffic that the town centre endured during daytime business hours. One can easily imagine just how gridlocked the streets within the heart of the town must have been at rush hour. It's equally wonderful to see the range of now classic cars and commercial vehicles illustrated here. Even with the busy traffic-filled streets, those who lived in Ashford through the 1960s still say that the town 'ran like clockwork'. (Bryan Sales)

Upper High Street, 1964. Another picture showing traffic flow in the Upper High Street, this time with an East Kent double-decker bus negotiating right of way with a lorry belonging to 1960s and '70s supermarket chain Pricerite, whose stores were in the Lower High Street. (Bryan Sales)

Upper High Street, 1964. Street-side parking and shop awnings appear to be the trend in this view where tailgating traffic sees this lorry a little bit too close for comfort with the van (centre and right). (Bryan Sales)

Upper High Street, 1964. Cars utilising the traffic island in a 'merry go round' fashion in a bid to negotiate this important and much-utilised junction. (Bryan Sales)

Upper High Street junction with Bank Street, 1964. This superb view shows the arterial Bank Street together with its queuing cars, lorries and buses, in a street which has not seen traffic like this since. Now one way in the direction of the High Street, it's difficult to comprehend today how these huge buses ever negotiated the narrow streets further through the town. Several old Ashfordians have spoken of near misses when it comes to buses versus buildings. One lady once told me that she used to hold her breath while sitting in the Mocha Bar in Middle Row as the buses used to get rather too close when turning into the Lower High Street. (Bryan Sales)

Upper High Street, September 1963. Former long-term mainstays of the Upper High Street, here we can see Geerings printers and stationers at no. 80 High Street (during a period when printing was still done on this site) and Hilton & Sons boot and shoe retailer at no. 78 with Burton tailoring just creeping into view on the right. Now Tesco Metro and Shoe Zone respectively, the Geerings premises has seen the biggest alteration. The illustrated post-war modern corrugated frontage to the upper elevation hid an earlier Geerings frontage where a large window was revealed during conversion and division to become Tesco. The window will be remembered in past times for being used as an advertising space for Imperial Typewriters. Note the Franco-type AA diversion sign fixed to the 'Keep Left' bollard outside Burton. (Bryan Sales)

Upper High Street, September 1963. A splendid view showing the recently departed chain of Burton tailoring (as it was known during this period) at nos 74–76. The firm was established in 1903 by Montague Maurice Burton (born Lithuanian Jew Meshe David Osinsky), who started as a pedlar and by 1913 Montague Burton had five shops. As far as the Ashford store was concerned, owners Arcadia Group chose not to renew the lease on the building which had fallen into a dreadful state of disrepair and had to be refurbished before becoming a café in 2018. (Bryan Sales)

Upper High Street, September 1963. Originally known as Timothy Whites and Taylors, Timothy Whites – pictured here at nos 70–72 – also occupied nos 60–62 and at one period took over the business of Mence Smith at no. 23 Bank Street. The Timothy Whites name was dissolved into the Boots the Chemist empire in the early 1980s. The premises illustrated had at one time been Boots in the 1970s after moving from nos 60–62, which, as mentioned above, had coincidentally also been Timothy Whites at one time. Following Sainsbury's vacating their premises at no. 56 High Street to move to their new store in Park Street, Boots took over their former store in September 1979. Nos 70–72 became Boots Cookshop for a time, before the premises were demolished for a new WHSmith store that opened in 1987. (Bryan Sales)

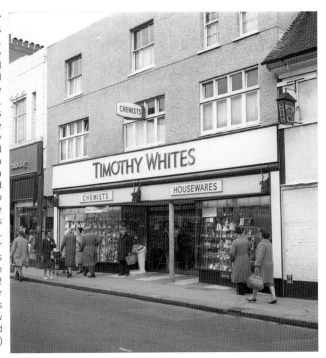

High Street (Middle), September 1963. More recognisable today as Barclays Bank and Iceland, nos 64–66 were purpose built for Marks & Spencer, which opened on this site in 1934. This handsome building, which at the time had 'Marks and Spencer Ltd' affixed to the stonework of the upper elevation, backs onto Park Street. The upper floors to the rear were home to the Donut Club, and American Red Cross dugout where American GIs proved an attraction to local girls. In 1978, Marks & Spencer moved to a new larger unit at the Tufton Centre and it wasn't until 1982 – after conversion works – that their former High Street premises became Barclays Bank on the upper floors and Cordon Bleu frozen foods on much of the ground floor, the latter being taken over by the Iceland chain in the 1990s. (Bryan Sales)

High Street (Kings Parade), September 1963. This dominant building within the centre of the upper and lower High Street known as Kings Parade, was for many years notable for housing the fire station in one section and the council chambers of Ashford Urban District Council. Of course many will also recall the public conveniences situated below. During the late 1950s, conversion work was undertaken on the building to accommodate retail space. In the early 1960s, stores such as Milletts of St Albans (the business having since dropped one of the Ts in their name to be known simply as Millets), camping gear and clothiers, opened at no. 3, with Little Folk, babywear, also trading next door from no. 2a. At a time when renting a television was an option and indeed a trend, Rentaset Limited offered just that at no. 2 (centre right). (Bryan Sales)

High Street (Kings Parade), September 1963. Despite the impending works to replace the ancient sewers in the High Street, it's business as usual with a rather unimpressed-looking lady sharing the street scene with a workman using a pneumatic drill. It's rather odd to see the lack of cordons between pedestrian and the work being undertaken and indeed, his lack of safety gear which is today a mandatory requirement. For many years, the showrooms of the South Eastern Electricity Board (Seeboard) were situated at the far end of Kings Parade at no. 5 until they moved to the Park Mall Shopping Centre in 1987. Next door, Advance Dry Cleaning at no. 4 became the town office of the *Kentish Express* newspaper in the 1980s. (Bryan Sales)

High Street (Middle), September 1963. A splendid period view illustrating the crammed windows of Boots the Chemist at nos 60–62 High Street and in one of three different trading locations in the same street during their presence in Ashford. It is interesting to note that this was a time when Boots had a highly sought after film processing service, something that seems to have slackened off in recent times. Another interesting point is that Boots advertise themselves as 'Toilet Specialists' in this 1963 view, a term that would likely cause confusion with shoppers today. (Bryan Sales)

High Street (Middle), 1969. Modern signage and streamlined window displays have replaced the uniform look of Boots on the High Street in the previous view. Two longstanding major chains on the High Street nowadays is something of a rarity. The town centre has recently lost its Marks & Spencer, and although reports state that Ashford isn't on the list of Boots' national closures and restructure for the moment, sadly often decisions are known to change, blowing previous assurances out of the water. (Steve Salter Archive)

High Street (Middle), September 1963. Back in the 1960s, there were many more independent grocers and provision merchants to choose from. Trading successfully for many years alongside the likes of the national chains which had also come to the town – such as Sainsbury's, International Stores and Pricerite – as these chains grew and offered a bigger discount, the shopper gradually turned their back on the independent counter-service stores in favour of their modern self-service counterparts which were in their infancy at this period. Even to this day, small independents try to offer a substitute to these once much-loved independents, but the level service doesn't come close. This view illustrates Kent independent grocer Vye and Son's store at no. 58, which traded successfully in the town until the end of the 1960s. (Bryan Sales)

High Street (Middle), 1969. A traffic warden keeps his beady eye on motorists in this view showing an array of classic motors negotiating the High Street before they were totally banned. Colour imagery often gives a false sense of modernity, but it's plain to see that times are changing on the High Street when comparing the scene with earlier views. Seeboard still dominates Kings Parade at this time, with few changed trades to be seen elsewhere. Ruffle Brothers menswear at no. 73 is visible in the background, a name that disappeared in the 1980s. (Steve Salter Archive)

High Street (Middle), September 1963. The fate of the one-time Saracen's Head Hotel had already been sealed when this scene was photographed, judging by the fact it was taken as part of a survey of the town's buildings. The beautiful and historic Courage-owned hostelry was of substantial proportions and had rooms for functions and a separate bar named Saracen's Head Shades. When placed up for sale for prospective redevelopment offers in December 1966, the former hotel was snapped up by Sainsbury's for £142,500 and the heritage asset was subsequently demolished to make way for the chain's first self-service store in the town. This development could be seen as an unfair act for next-door neighbour grocer Vye and Son, who were probably forced out by the move. (Bryan Sales)

High Street junction with Bank Street, 1968. A rare colour shot showing the early days of the first Sainsbury's self-service store at no. 56 High Street, where the Saracen's Head Hotel once stood. Taken outside of the renowned Mocha Bar, one can see that Vye's at no. 58 has indeed closed at this point: they wouldn't have stood a chance of trading successfully with a bright, modern new supermarket next door. (Steve Salter Archive)

CHAPTER 2

CALM BEFORE
THE STORM

High Street junction with North Street, September 1963. Considering that no. 54 (illustrated) has been a Grade II listed property since September 1951, a recent trend and lack of enforcement by authorities has seen this heritage asset of importance allowed to deteriorate and find itself as a candidate for a local 'heritage at risk' register. Owned for many years by Arcadia Group, whose subsidiary Evans occupied it for many years, when challenged, they claimed that they couldn't afford to look after the building, and since Evans' departure, the building has been sub-let for questionable choices of usage. For many years, John Collier the once well-known men's outfitter occupied the building. No. 54, which was originally constructed in about 1680 as a grand town house, had previously been occupied by Thomas Coulthard the draper in the nineteenth century. (Bryan Sales)

High Street junction with North Street, 1969. Again, modernity has set in with a vengeance. A simple and unsightly shop front typical of the mid-1960s has replaced the period shop front and classical pillars present in previous times. Fashions have also changed in a scene which could be mistaken for a 1980s shot. Further along, at no. 46, Headley grocer can be seen (centre right) had a dominant presence in the town from 1848 and purchased no. 36 when business was originally established. The grocery business moved to Cobbs Wood in around 1974 and the vacant premises were rebuilt in the same style and opened as Headley Brothers retail bookshop, stationer and post office, which traded from this prime location until 1988. The separate printing business established in 1881 was put up for sale in 2017 and acquired by Oxfordshire printer Stones, which bought Headley's out of administration. Sadly, by December, Stones collapsed with debts of nearly £4.2 million resulting in scores of job losses. The printer's Queens Road site has since largely been demolished. (Steve Salter Archive)

Lower High Street, September 1963. Cycles were certainly a popular form of transport in this nostalgic view illustrating nos 48, 50 and 52 High Street. The upper elevation of these properties has certainly had a mismatch of treatments over the years by the unsympathetic addition of shopfronts obscuring the upper floors. Although owned by several different proprietors over the decades, the newsagents is still called The Chocolate Box at the time of writing in 2019. Linda's Florist replaced Dewhurst the butcher, a brand first seen in the UK in 1905 that entered administration 90 years later and occupied no fewer than four different sites in the town during the company's existence. Boyd's of Bond Street, radio and television, disappeared in the mid-1970s and the premises were then, for many years, occupied by clothier Stranges (where most Ashfordians' school uniforms came from) owned by Bryan Strange and his family. Today Mr Simms's old-fashioned sweet shop occupies the site. (Bryan Sales)

Lower High Street, September 1963. A wonderful view illustrating the former grocery business of Headley at no. 46 and prior to their moving to wholesale and relocating to Cobbs Wood. Locals remember Headley's with much affection and will recall the deliveries at the shop being taken through the gate at the side on tracks like those used on a railway. Today the dominant retail space is occupied by a branch of McDonalds and has been since 1989. One thing to come out of the redevelopment of no. 46 is that the Pitt family, who owned the business, rescued the illustrated gates and placed them on a rear entrance created by the firm – namely Chapel Mews. The post office and stationery shop of Headley Brothers, which later moved into no. 46, can be seen creeping into view on the right. (Bryan Sales)

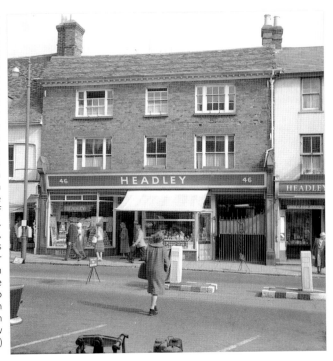

Lower High Street, September 1963. Shared space – it's business as usual in this view showing the Headley Brothers premises at no. 44 with J. Ingall & Son chemist at no. 42, Salon Margaret above at 42a and Photocraft at no. 40. Today, workers would not get away with the lack of protection given to pedestrians as illustrated. The upper floors of no. 42 occupied then by the salon and latterly Keith R.A. Skinner, optician, are currently being converted into flats. (Bryan Sales)

Lower High Street, September 1963. A simple rope separates shoppers from the ongoing works in this splendid view illustrating nos 36, 38 and Photocraft at no. 40. Many Ashfordians will recall long-lost business such as Marsh the Seedsman at no. 36, a business that traded into the mid-1970s, with Beasley dyers and cleaners at no. 38; a firm that became Kengate-Beasley in the 1970s and still trades as Kengate at South Stour Avenue in 2019. It's interesting to note that Photocraft owner Victor Mathews used the left-hand side of no. 38 (with no sign) for his tape recorder department during this period. Nos 36 and 38 were rebuilt for Headley's post office and toy shop when they moved from further up the street in the late 1970s. (Bryan Sales)

Lower High Street, September 1963. One wonders if those waiting for the bus behind the rope are expected to do the limbo dance in order to board the vehicle in this view illustrating the Ashford Co-operative Society electrical department and tobacconist at nos 32 and 34 respectively. Bateman's opticians can be seen on the immediate right at no. 30; it traded from the site and in the town for many years. (Bryan Sales)

Lower High Street, September 1963. A period view showing Bateman's premises at no. 30 High Street, sandwiched between the electrical department and department store of Ashford Co-operative Society. (Bryan Sales)

Lower High Street, September 1963. 'Road Works Ahead' – the street scene and appearance of this section of the Lower High Street has changed considerably since the early 1960s, with several of the illustrated buildings having been demolished – even those on the far left at the junction of East Hill and Station Road, the latter being removed for the construction of the Ringway. The taller building with the white upper elevation, together with two neighbouring buildings coming up the High Street, were demolished in 1968 to make way for new offices for insurance firm Pearl Assurance. At this time, nos 1, 3, 3a and 5 were occupied by Alfred Olby Limited, wallpaper and paint, Rediffusion cable television rentals and the builder's merchant and ironmongery department of Alfred Olby. Further up the street (centre right), the tall building with the ornate gable occupied here J.R. Kempe-Roberts, dental surgeon, at no. 17, Keith R.A. Skinner, optician, at no. 17a and Cameron Rainwear at 17b were also demolished to make way for three shops. (Bryan Sales)

Lower High Street, August 1963. Previously the site of Lees bedding centre (their main shop was at the bottom of the High Street at nos 4–8), long-since dissolved supermarket chain Pricerite pictured here at no. 22 had this modern, typically 1960s-style replacement shop purpose built for their use. The new store was barely open at the time of this picture being taken. Almost five years later, following the redevelopment by Pricerite of the Lees site at nos 4–8, the chain relocated their supermarket there and utilised the store illustrated here for their 'Wear and Ware' department. Many will remember that no. 22 was for many years the home of the Job Centre. (Bryan Sales)

Lower High Street, August 1963. Still dominant in the same premises today, NatWest, seen here in an earlier guise as Westminster Bank, is one of the very few banking institutions in the town that has relocated. The handsome premises at no. 20 replaced a previous building occupied by the London and County Bank. Over the decades the premises have been altered both externally and internally and during the 1980s the former neighbouring counter-service Sainsburys branch at no. 18 was combined with the bank. Following a merger with National Provincial Bank, which was first suggested in 1968, Westminster Bank became National Westminster Bank by 1970, a name that was abbreviated to NatWest in the 1990s. (Bryan Sales)

Lower High Street, August 1963. Disguised by its sun awning, this picture illustrates the original counter-service store of Sainsburys at no. 18 High Street, adjacent to ladies' independent clothier Marshalls Fashions at no. 16. The Sainsbury's store first opened on the site in 1934 and was decorated internally with mosaic floors and Minton tiled walls – the company's uniform design. Following the chain's move in 1968 to a new self-service store at no. 56 High Street (now Boots), no. 18 became a charity shop for a few years before being taken over by the bank. During a refurbishment in 1991, the Minton-tiled walls were discovered behind plasterboard and wallpaper. Marshalls, which had the same owner as Victor's Fashions in Bank Street, closed in around 1976. (Bryan Sales)

Lower High Street, August 1963. Further to the right and now occupied by a Cancer Research charity shop, this view shows the one-time Ideal hairdressing salon at no. 14, which existed in the town for generations, latterly trading on the upper floor of the premises. It was at this location, believed to be the premises of Marshalls, that the Modern High School for Girls was founded in 1898 by the Reverend Thimann and his wife Muriel. Today the school is better known as Ashford School and dominates the entirety of East Hill. (Bryan Sales)

Lower High Street, August 1963. A wonderful window display adorns the premises of Halford Cycle Co. Ltd at no. 12 High Street adjacent to the County Hotel (pictured right). Founded by Frederick Rushbrooke in 1892 as a wholesale ironmongery, the chain was initially renowned for its town centre stores like the one illustrated here. It opened its 300th store in 1968. Although named 'Cycle Co.', the company quickly expanded into automotive accessories, and today the company's town-centre stores have been replaced by out-of-town retail units and, in the last few years, repair centres. The Ashford High Street store closed in the mid-1990s to be initially replaced by a large store at the Warren Retail Park, but following the enlargement of neighbouring Sainsbury's, the store was relocated to Norman Road after the plans saw the Warren store acquired for demolition. Few will be aware that, during the 1960s, former Prime Minister Margaret Thatcher's husband Denis was a non-executive director of the company. (Bryan Sales)

Lower High Street, August 1963. A group of workmen and officials investigate a large and unguarded trench outside the County Hotel during the replacement of the dilapidated sewer system in the Lower High Street while a passing motorist negotiates safely through. Again, there are no precautionary measures in place to protect the workforce or indeed anyone leaving the County. The former hotel, previously known as the Fernley Commercial and Temperance Hotel, was converted into a Wetherspoons in 1998 and, during its time as a hotel, was known for its sprung dancefloor in the ballroom at the rear. (Bryan Sales)

Lower High Street, 1969. This splendid view illustrates the Lower High Street at the end of the 1960s when many of the business and trades that we remember with fondness were still present. There is an array of old-fashioned vehicles for the avid vintage motor enthusiast to identify. The gap on the left shows that the former premises of Alfred Olby at no. 1, Handover Bros, outfitter, at no. 3, Rediffusion South-East at no. 3a and Alfred Olby builders merchants and ironmongers at no. 5, have been demolished at this point to make way for new district offices for Pearl Assurance. Further along the street, nos 17, 17a and 17b have been demolished and replaced with three new shop units. They had previously been home of J.R. Kempe-Roberts, dentist, Keith R.A. Skinner, optician, and Cameron Rainwear respectively. The Co-operative grocery and butchery store can be seen on the left at nos 7, 9 and 11, with Martins Bank (shortly before its rebranding and amalgamation with Barclays) at no. 13, which was previously the home of nurserymen and florist Florifruit. (Bryan Sales)

Lower High Street junction with Station Road and Wellesley Road, 1967. One forgets how narrow this junction was in previous times compared with today, especially the way that the Ringway now carves through this section now. Everything in view was either demolished for the Ringway or, in Olby's case (centre), demolished for Pearl Assurance House, today known as Northdown House. (Bryan Sales)

Lower High Street, August 1963. One of the doomed premises of Olby's at no. 5 are seen here a few years before destruction in the name of progress took place. The premises had at one time been an ancient hotel called the Royal Oak. (Bryan Sales)

Lower High Street, August 1963. More familiar today as a Kentucky Fried Chicken and independent restaurant Namuna, nos 7, 9 and 11 are seen here during alterations by the Co-operative to improve its grocery department. The premises have seen a whole range of tenants since the departure of the Co-op in the 1980s, which include a wallpaper and paint specialist, a sports shop and a carpet shop. Florifruit florist and nurserymen can be seen just creeping into view on the right. (Bryan Sales)

Lower High Street, August 1963. Latterly Martins Bank (until 1969 when it was taken over by Barclays Bank), florist Florifruit is seen here during its time in the High Street with Soundcraft next door at no. 15. No. 15 had previously been the home of Doughtys tobacconist for many years. The Soundcraft shop was an early incarnation of the business run by Geoff Mathews at no. 40, previously known as Photocraft Hi-fi and now known as Soundcraft Hi-Fi. The business was established by Geoff's father, the respected businessman Victor Mathews. (Bryan Sales)

Lower High Street, August 1963. These substantial and ornate-gabled premises, midway along the south side of the High Street, for many years housed the businesses of J.R. Kempe-Roberts, dentist, optician Keith R.A. Skinner and Cameron Rainwear (pictured) at nos 17, 17a and 17b. In a prime example of sacrilegious planning, the local authority allowed the demolition of this beautiful building, together with the neighbouring premises of Soundcraft at no. 15, to be replaced by three shops with first-floor accommodation. One wonders why planners allowed such destructive acts to go ahead back then. (Bryan Sales)

Lower High Street, August 1963. Freshly ground coffee was one of several once-familiar smells that Ashfordians would connect with C.F. Hutson's grocery at no. 19. Hutson's was one of many independent grocers in the town for shoppers to choose from. The larger incoming players into the town, such as the chains that were continually undercutting the independent, eventually made business for the likes of Hutson's unsustainable. This particular business closed in 1973, with no. 19 making way for the first Wimpy bar in the town which opened in 1974 and traded here until the 1990s. (Bryan Sales)

Lower High Street, August 1963. Next door, decorating specialist Globe Wallpapers at no. 21 for many years traded beside the much-missed Bon at no. 23, run by the respected Matassa family. The Bon became a kebab shop in the 1990s with neighbouring Globe Wallpapers becoming the home of Antoniou hairdressers, which have branches in other places in Kent such as Canterbury and Faversham. (Bryan Sales)

Lower High Street, 1969. A nostalgic view taken nearly six years later, showing the Bon and its neighbours in this long-forgotten street scene. Further along the south side, the Leek and Westbourne Building Society at no. 25 sits proudly with its Kent Invicta horse ensign on the front gable of the building. The wonderful Gizzi restaurant can be easily picked out at no. 29. Owned and operated by hugely respected couple Vilma and Antonio 'Tony' Gizzi, locals had much affection for the husband and wife team and their lovely staff. After surviving her husband for several years following his untimely passing, Vilma sadly died in 2018 after a short illness. Next door at no. 31, also known as St John's Chambers, stands estate agent Scott and Kendon where historian the late Richard Filmer started in the trade as a 17-year-old. At the time, Betabake occupied part of the ground floor, space which was eventually taken over by the estate agency in the years that followed. The 1936-built Odeon cinema can be seen further along (centre right) with Midland Bank at no. 39 and chain International Stores (temporarily occupying) no. 41 respectively. International had temporarily relocated to the former premises of G.V. Crump, grocer, as a new larger store was being built on the site of their permanent base a no. 92. (Steve Salter)

Lower High Street, August 1963. An earlier view of no. 31 shows Victoria Wine and Kingfield Bakeries operating from part of the premises largely occupied by Scott, Kendon and Ronald Pearce. Richard Filmer once told me that the sign in the roof parapet, which had also been the positioning of the signage when no. 31 was occupied by Fendall's wine merchant, was ordered to be removed by the local authority after standing unchallenged for years. The footpath to Vicarage Lane car park can be seen on the immediate right. In recent times and while an estate agency, comedians Vic Reeves and Bob Mortimer rented space on the upper floors of no. 31. After Ronald Pearce left the business at the end of the 1960s, the respected estate agency changed its name to Scott and Kendon in 1969. (Bryan Sales)

Lower High Street, 1969. A splendid view looking towards Middle Row with the Upper High Street clearly visible in the distance. The Odeon ceased its life as a cinema in 1976 and became a bingo hall until recent owners Mecca pulled out of the town in 2018. With the former cinema and bingo hall purchased by Ashford Borough Council, plans have been revealed by the authority to part demolish the building, notably the auditorium, as they feel it 'obscures the view of the church'. Not satisfied with that, historians, preservation societies and local people put in an application in 2019 to list the building, to assist in halting the ultimate destruction illustrated in the plans set forward. It is largely felt by Ashfordians that to pedestrianise the lower High Street was a mistake and that the bus stops and passing trade were key to the sustainability of this part of town in years past. (Steve Salter Archive)

Lower High Street, August 1963. With the street looking like the obstacle course on ITV's *The Krypton Factor* during works to replace the sewage system, this view shows the Odeon together with its two shop units beneath, notably occupied by James Walker, jeweller, and latterly H. Samuel of the same trade for many years. It's great to see pictures of the Odeon during its years of operation and to see the billboards advertising the movies being screened. In this view *Jason and the Argonauts* and *Siege of the Saxons* (both 1963 films) are showing at the once-popular venue. (Bryan Sales)

Lower High Street, August 1963. Many Ashfordians of a certain age will fondly reminisce when seeing this wonderful image illustrating grocer, provision merchant and butcher G.V. Crump at no. 41 with Midland Bank at no. 39 next door to the left. Crump's will be remembered for their high standards in service and their splendid displays of grocery, butchery and provision items. The likes of such displays are a rarity nowadays with uniform displays and the uniqueness and character of the independent trader largely absent. Midland Bank latterly expanded their bank into no. 41 and became HSBC in the mid-1990s. Kennington Laundry can be seen creeping into view (right) at no. 41a in a newer building which replaced those occupied by G. Stevenson, greengrocer and fishmonger – what a combination! (Bryan Sales)

Lower High Street, 1969. Absent from the street scene of this period, the premises of Alfred Olby, Handover Brothers and Rediffusion have been demolished at this point (centre) as Hoskins tobacconist at no. 2 East Hill and Tiffany's café at no. 3 Station Road are clearly visible at the bottom of the High Street. Works have yet to commence on the impending construction of Pearl Assurance House at the site. The Lower High Street, reputed to be one of the widest in the country, is largely deserted today and is pedestrianised. It's hard to believe how busy the street was not that many years ago and that the livestock market was held in this part of the High Street in times past – as depicted in artist George Sidney Shepherd's famous painting of the town. It is the opinion of many local people that the Lower High Street should be restored to the way it was as illustrated here. Note the array of old cars in this splendid view. (Steve Salter Archive)

Lower High Street, August 1963. Research identifies this part-fourteenth-century building as the 'marketplace' in earlier generations and during renovations in the early 1980s an carved oak window of medieval design was found, suggesting it was a building of some importance – probably as some sort of market hall. There is also evidence that the building, in its sheltered spot, was where the market traders would erect their stalls in the 1500s. Years later, the 'hall' was divided and converted for use as shops as illustrated. Back in 1963, Sercombe's menswear and school shop, the much-loved Mocha Bar and Leavers tobacconist were mainstays of this building's occupancy. Sercombe's (pictured) can be seen here during a time at which regulations were slack when it came to advertising your business on buildings of historical merit such as those that are listed or in conservation area. This building was Grade II listed in September 1951. Authorities set rulings for a time in the 1980s and '90s, but now don't seem to be all that bothered. The taller building behind had been the telephone exchange in years gone by. (Bryan Sales)

High Street (Middle Row), August 1963. Many Ashfordians still recall the Mocha Bar in Middle Row and how business was always brisk back then. Cafés and restaurants in the town were numerous in the 1960s, and they all had something unique to offer. Today, respected estate agent Nigel Gould operates Gould Harrison from the former Mocha Bar. The upstairs restaurant area is now its lettings department and until 2017, part of the first floor was used for the office of the late Richard Filmer a partner in the business and veteran of some 54 years at his untimely passing. (Bryan Sales)

High Street (Middle Row), August 1963. A wonderful picture looking at the heart of Middle Row with its narrow thoroughfares leading to the church of St Mary the Virgin. The building in the centre was built in 1877 and is seen here with Doughtys tobacconist occupying no. 2 and Bartlett and Best saddler at no. 2a respectively. The vintage road signage and traffic light design really give a feel for the era. The picture, taken from North Street, also shows the premises of electrical engineer G.E. Wallis creeping into view (right). (Bryan Sales)

CHAPTER 3

TOWN OF TRANQUILITY

High Street junction with North Street, September 1963. From as early as the 1400s there has been an inn bearing the name of the Saracen's Head on the prominent site at the junctions of North Street and High Street. Substantial alterations were made to the earlier property in 1862. At one point in history, this was the site of the Manor House of Ashford, which at its peak had 150 tenants. In later years, the hotel was owned by Courage and in December 1966, the hotel and site went to auction, selling to Sainsbury's for £142,500. The supermarket chain commissioned Messrs Epps of Ashford to construct the company's first self-service supermarket for the town. (Bryan Sales)

North Street junction with High Street, September 1963. The imposing Victorian architecture of the Saracen's Head is seen here from North Street during the works to replace the sewage system in the town centre. (Bryan Sales)

North Street, September 1963. An extremely rare view showing Mascotts confectioner and tobacconist premises beside of Saracen's Head Hotel at no. 1. The yard entrance to the hotel is pictured (centre right). (Bryan Sales)

North Street, September 1963. This rather obscure view shows the rear of the Saracen's Head Hotel at the junction of North Street and Park Street with A.E. Marson fruit and vegetables, Jacksons hairdresser and Josephine hair fashions at nos 3 and 3a respectively. Today, there is no trace of the hotel or indeed these buildings ever having existed at all. (Bryan Sales)

High Street junction with North Street, September 1963. An atmospheric view illustrating North Street where it meets the High Street, at a time when this part of the town was still used as a through route from the A28 between Ashford and Canterbury. Two once-familiar shops that are no longer in business today can be seen – Ashley Russell milliners and costumiers at no. 2 North Street with John Collier outfitters at no. 54 High Street. Both traders, which operated multiple stores in the United Kingdom, ceased to exist by the early 1980s. Ashley Russell also had stores in Ilford, Kingston and Hammersmith. John Collier had originally traded under the 'Fifty Shilling Tailor' brand, but after the company was sold to the United Drapery Stores empire in 1958, the company was named John Collier and then used thereafter. The company eventually disappeared in 1985 after being sold onto the Burton Group and the brand was discontinued. (Bryan Sales)

North Street, September 1963. Window displays of eras such as the 1950s and '60s were quite often memorable and unlike anything we see today. Huge effort was given to this type of merchandising in previous decades, as illustrated in this splendid view. Here we see multiple window displays surrounding the entrance to Ashley Russell, whose business traded from both the ground and upper floors. (Bryan Sales)

North Street, September 1963. It is not widely known beyond the town, but Ashford-born novelist, author and journalist Frederick Forsyth's parents ran F. & P. Forsyth furriers and costumiers at no. 4 for many years (pictured). Famous for his espionage novels *The Day of the Jackal* and *The Odessa File*, Forsyth was born in the town in 1938 and in 1956 joined the *Kentish Express* as a rookie reporter, before being called up for National Service. The yard entrance of Denne seed merchants can be seen on the left, with the entrance to Headley grocer's yard (centre right) and adjacent to Ashley Russell. (Bryan Sales)

North Street, September 1963. Successors to Hart and Tatnall who occupied the same trade and premises, here we can see the familiar premises of one-time corn and seed merchants Denne at nos 6, 8 and 10 North Street with the yard to rear. Denne's operated successfully from these premises for generations before closing their retail business (pictured) and their other shop next door in around 1990. Firstly, Supersaver Discount Stores took over the premises – which had been built in 1883 – and then Top Notch, another discount store, followed. In December 1997, a huge blaze occurred at Top Notch which was reported to have started in the sub-let carpet shop to the rear, all but destroying the local landmark. For ten years, the shell of the building stood empty, before being rebuilt and converted into a Chinese restaurant. (Bryan Sales)

North Street, September 1963. The main Denne's shop at no. 6 North Street with the long-lost Lord Roberts public house on the immediate left. The ancient hostelry, previously called the Red Lion, was demolished in 1972 to make way for a service road upon the construction of Charter House. (Bryan Sales)

Somerset Road, October 1962. An extremely rare view taken at the junction of Somerset Road and Wellesley Road taken in the days before the construction of Mace Lane. Until 1971, Mace Lane was a dirt track where properties locally known as 'black huts' were situated and used by local people. Firstly, the road was built at the position illustrated for traffic travelling towards Hythe Road, but traffic still had to come up East Hill for nearly three more years until the town-bound side of Mace Lane was built. This was carried out in conjunction with the new Ringway. (Bryan Sales)

Somerset Road (Mace Lane), October 1962. Another survey picture showing the unmade Mace Lane, prior to a proper road being built. Years later, some of the land on which the huts and track once stood was used as allotments. A crane and piling rig can be seen in the background (right) which indicates the start of the Mace Industrial Estate development. The black huts have long gone by this point in time. (Bryan Sales)

47

Wellesley Road, July 1963. In a part of the town where substantial changes have taken place and prior to the destruction of Somerset and Wellesley Roads for the Ringway and triple-winged office block Charter House, these houses stood along the south side of Somerset Road and are seen here from the rear. In the days before the road scheme, Somerset Road was considerably narrower compared to how it is today. The continuation of Wellesley Road can be picked out in the background (extreme right) of the picture. (Bryan Sales)

Somerset Road junction with Wellesley Road, July 1963. This time, the houses are seen from the front, looking along Wellesley Road towards the side of County Components premises and the rear of the Lower High Street. (Bryan Sales)

Wellesley Road, June 1963. These lovely houses, nos 18, 20, 22, 24, 26, 28 and 32 Wellesley Road, were for many years used as staff hostel accommodation for staff and teachers at Ashford School in nearby East Hill, while no. 30 was the premises of Queen's Nurse – Midwives and Home Nurses (Kent County Council) Midwives. The houses, that backed onto the school's tennis courts, were subsequently demolished for the Ringway in 1972. A sign adjacent to the picket fencing (left) identifies the entrance to Paul I. Headley's British Wheel Works, a short time before the Crouch family purchased the business two years later in 1965 and moved operations to Dover Place. (Bryan Sales)

Wellesley Road, June 1963. Another view clearly showing the houses and proximity to Lee and Son's warehouse, while the surveyor's mate strikes up a conversation with a passer-by. (Bryan Sales)

Wellesley Road, July 1963. Residents of this locality will recall this public footpath which ran from Wellesley Road up to Somerset Road – its entrance beside Keen's Stores. The said footpath disappeared following the construction of Charter House, but, while in existence, divided the large garden of no. 22 North Street, the home of the locally known Lepard sisters. (Bryan Sales)

Wellesley Road, July 1963. This entrance at the side of County Components' premises once served the rear of properties in the Lower High Street in the days prior to a permanent distributor road and extension to Park Street being built. This necessitated the demolition of ancient hostelry the Lord Roberts in North Street, causing anger and controversy among local residents. The new road was operational by 1975. (Bryan Sales)

Wellesley Road, July 1963. The service entrance to the rear of the Lower High Street and the footpath to Somerset Road (centre). Today there is absolutely no trace of this street scene remaining whatsoever. County Components can be seen on the left. (Bryan Sales)

Wellesley Road, July 1963. Some of the many properties no longer in existence in the street and that fell foul of the redevelopment plans. Here we can see nos 13a–15, which were largely used for business in the 1960s. (Bryan Sales)

Wellesley Road, July 1963. While the buildings either side of electric meter manufacturer Emetco's premises at no. 11 were eventually demolished, the business premises was the last to go in this once-familiar row of properties. Those buildings to the left at nos 7–9 and 9a were demolished for a new Pricerite supermarket in 1968, and those buildings to the left were knocked down in 1973 in readiness for the new service road. (Bryan Sales)

Wellesley Road, July 1963. A rare and splendid view illustrating the premises of Bligh Brothers Limited (Central Garage) at no. 9a Wellesley Road with Emetco further along on the right. The goods entrance to furnisher Lee and Son's premises in the High Street can be seen on the immediate left of the picture. (Bryan Sales)

Wellesley Road, July 1963. One cannot believe how narrow the town centre street was here compared with today. This wonderfully nostalgic picture is a far cry from today's hustle bustle and will give residents who remember the town of the past, plenty of reason to hanker after a calmer and gentler era. The offices and showroom of furnisher Lee and Son can be seen (centre left) with the side of the one-time premises of Pearks Stores at no. 2 High Street on the immediate left. (Bryan Sales)

Wellesley Road, June 1963. A month earlier, this surveyor's image shows that the former premises of Pearks Stores at no. 2 High Street at its junction with Wellesley Road is already empty. There was quite a characterful mismatch of different buildings in this part of town at the time. Note the lovely Kellogg's Corn Flakes advert affixed to the side wall of the former Pearks premises. (Bryan Sales)

Wellesley Road, June 1963. A somewhat rare and forgotten view of Lee and Son's furniture store and one-time auction rooms locally known as 'Wellesley Hall', one of several adjoining buildings that had been used generations earlier as 'The Original Brewery' started by brewster and maltster Walter M. Richardson. Many of the larger buildings on the site, including a large chimney, had already long disappeared at this time. These surviving buildings were eventually to be demolished in the years that followed. (Bryan Sales)

Wellesley Road, June 1963. Further to the right of the previous picture, we see another part of the former brewery buildings known as Wellesley Hall, where Lee's advertise 'Removals and Warehousing' on the side of the building. (Bryan Sales)

Wellesley Road, June 1963. Another view illustrating the former buildings of 'The Original Brewery', while being used by Lee and Son, furnishers. An illustration in the local book *Rochard's Ashford* shows the substantial presence that the brewer had on the site. It's sad to think that buildings of such relevance and that are key to the heritage of the town were sacrificed for a road scheme. (Bryan Sales)

Wellesley Road, June 1963. This somewhat ramshackle but quaint property to the rear of the Duke of Marlborough public house at the corner of East Hill and Wellesley Road was known locally as 'The Cottage'. Standing at no. 2, at this time it was used as the stores for the nearby business of Alfred Olby Ltd, whose premises were based in the lower High Street. There are very faint traces of signage painted on the exterior of the property, but these are sadly impossible to decipher. Watney's were until recently a name that had faded into history, however at the time of writing crowdfunding efforts have seen the brand revived by a trio of entrepreneurs with a love and respect for traditional brewing. (Bryan Sales)

Wellesley Road, June 1963. Further towards the junction with East Hill and Station Road, here we can see the rear of the Duke of Marlborough public house together with the neighbouring property belonging to Ashford School known as 'The Refuge', at nos 5–7 East Hill. The latter property is still standing today, but the ornate hostelry with its turreted corner was sacrificed for the Ringway construction. (Bryan Sales)

Wellesley Road, June 1963. A rarely pictured view showing the turreted corner of the Duke of Marlborough seen from the side elevation in Wellesley Road illustrating the entrance to the saloon bar. Ashford lost a number of watering holes through demolition back in the 1960s and '70s and the Duke was undoubtedly the most handsome buildings to be lost. Note the narrow streets at this section compared to today's wide expanse of tarmac. I know what I would rather see. (Bryan Sales)

East Hill junction with Wellesley Road, High Street and Station Road, June 1963. Few would disagree that the destruction of the one-time Watney's-owned Duke of Marlborough at the corner of East Hill and Wellesley Road was one of the most controversial elements of the reorganisation of Ashford during the 1960s and '70s. Even after all these years, historians and residents alike cannot understand the decisions made by our planning predecessors, which to robbed an area rich with heritage of a building of such architectural merit. Given that 'The Refuge' at the top of East Hill (right) is the only building still standing today, one wonders whether an incentive was in place for the planners? The former premises of Pearks Stores can be seen on the immediate left of the picture with Hoskin's tobacconist premises adjacent to the traffic lights (right). (Bryan Sales)

East Hill junction with Wellesley Road, High Street and Station Road, 1964. Despite the gridlock and bottlenecks of the town's narrow streets and junctions, here we see the doomed hostelry and neighbouring businesses within a setting typical of any weekday scene. There was no real need to build the Ringway so close the town's heart and historic area, but nevertheless it was, and locals have rued the decision ever since. (Bryan Sales)

East Hill junction with Wellesley Road, High Street and Station Road, 1964. A lorry belonging to local nearby business Alfred Olby Ltd goes head to head with a double-decker bus belonging to local operator East Kent Road Car Company, with another behind. A policeman 'referees' the potential jam, something that is seen as a rarity today, hence the regular gridlock on today's more modern roads. The tower of the 1901-built East Hill Mill can be picked out in the distance. (Bryan Sales)

East Hill junction with Wellesley Road, High Street and Station Road, 1964. A charming view showing a queuing row of bygone motor vehicles alongside residents calmly going about their daily routines. The surviving 'Refuge' can readily be picked out. (Bryan Sales)

Elwick Road junction with Station Road, 1964. In another part of town, traffic is still busy, but compared to today, these pre-Ringway views are in fact no worse than today's shambolic effort by highways chiefs. At least back then we didn't have to contend with two sets of traffic lights within 100 yards of each other! The Ashford Technical College and Juvenile Employment Bureau can be seen on the right, together with the Royal Mail sorting office, which was situated here until the late 1970s. Many residents will remember the Cottage and Cottage Shop fruit and flowers just visible further along on the left. (Bryan Sales)

Elwick Road junction with Station Road, 1964. Granted, there wasn't as much traffic on the roads back in 1964 compared to today, but nowadays traffic lights have an awful lot to answer for. Except for road widths and measurements, the highways authorities have basically returned the 1970s Ringway, back to as it was here. (Bryan Sales)

Elwick Road junction with Station Road, 1964. Many residents and users of buses in this bygone era will remember with fondness the double-decker buses operating in the town. During the 1960s the Kent Messenger Group newspaper advertised on the buses (note the 'KM') on the front of this one approaching the junction of Station Road. (Bryan Sales)

CHAPTER 4

A SENSE OF COMPLETENESS

Upper High Street junction with New Rents and Castle Street, 1962. A prime example of the sacrilegious decisions made by planners of the past to rid the town of large sections of its heritage. Today, there is no trace of this street scene, with everything in view being pulled down between 1972 and 1976 for phases 1 and 2 of the Tufton Shopping Centre development – the main section opening in 1975. Many long-term residents will remember these long-forgotten independents well, some of which had operated for generations. From left to right: Brickies of Kent Ltd butchers (at no. 109), with Frank Palmer outfitter next door (nos 111–13), then at the corner of Hempsted Street, Nicholas Kingsman bakers and confectioners operated for many years from nos 1–5 New Rents, with the imposing department store of Lewis and Hyland dominating the street at nos 7 and 9–19 respectively. (Bryan Sales)

Upper High Street junction with New Rents and Castle Street, 1962. A superb view illustrating a hostelry that survived well into the 1990s at its prime position within the town centre. The Shepherd Neame-owned Castle Hotel (latterly The Castle) at no. 1 Castle Street was one of the town's ancient watering holes and in later years was a regular venue for bikers. In 1996, The Castle closed its doors for the final time and the loyal and regular clientele followed popular licensees Delia and Stuart Barton firstly to the Victoria which became the Castle's replacement (until it too was demolished) and latterly to Oranges (the former Elephant and Castle) in Apsley Street, which itself closed a few years back. In 1997, the former Castle became a branch of Halifax building society. Many will fondly remember Jack Guy, pork butcher, next door (right) at no. 3. (Bryan Sales)

Castle Street, 1962. For many years, no. 3 has been the home to Topps Jewellers and prior to this it had been a greengrocer and a model shop. Jack Guy was one of several butchers in the town during this period, with H.J. Davis, another pork butcher, just around the corner in New Rents. Knowles toy and pram store can be seen further to the right at nos 5–7. (Bryan Sales)

Castle Street, 1962.
Knowles was a multi-departmental business in several locations around the vicinity of the Upper High Street, Castle Street and at one time New Street. Here we can see their carpet department at nos 6a, 8 and 10, with Watson's gentlemen's hair salon at no. 4a (centre), J.H. Broome, tobacconist, at no. 4 (centre right) and the separate snack bar of Crameri's Restaurant at no. 2. The premises occupied by Knowles (pictured) has since been demolished to provide a service area to the rear of shops in the Upper High Street. (Bryan Sales)

Castle Street junction with Park Street, 1962.
Another forgotten view of Knowles' premises in Castle Street together with its neighbouring TV and radio department at the corner of Park Street, also demolished in the name of progress. (Bryan Sales)

Park Street, July 1962.
During 1974, a widening project was undertaken in Park Street that saw a number of old and new buildings demolished on either side of the street including this modern late 1950s extension to the rear of drapery and milliners premises James and Kither at no. 104 High Street (pictured). The flat-roofed extension was built for proprietor Mr James to extend the shop which in part was Grade II listed at the High Street end of the premises. (Bryan Sales)

New Street/St George's Square, 1962.
Long parted from the neighbouring buildings through redevelopment and demolition, this rare image illustrates another of the town's surviving hostelries, The Old Prince of Wales in St Georges Square, at this time owned by Kent brewer Fremlins. In the late 1960s the neighbouring premises at no. 14 (left), once belonging to nearby Haywards Garage, were demolished and The Vineyard drive-through off-licence occupied the site for a number of years afterwards. (Bryan Sales)

New Street, 1962.
Remembered by generations
upon generations of
teenagers, this splendid
view illustrates the long-lost
Tank Milk bar at nos 3–5,
owned by much-respected
businessman Ted Collins.
Despite recessions in every
decade, such meeting
places were plentiful and
held their own financially
due to their popularity with
the loyal local customer
base. Today, business isn't
that easily sustainable, and
with rising overheads and
astronomical business rates
in the town, sadly more
and more of these meeting
places disappear. Goddard's
butcher can be seen
creeping into view on the left
with Daniel's estate agents
on the right. The Milk Bar
closed in the late 1970s and
was replaced by an Indian
restaurant. (Bryan Sales)

New Street, 1962. A
fantastic view showing
the estate agency of
Daniels at no. 7, with
neighbouring Goulden's
wools and fancy goods
at no. 9 (centre) and
Jack Scott's second-hand
bargain shop at no.
11. More casual attire
would be the norm
for window cleaners
nowadays, or perhaps
that's the suited estate
agent cleaning his own
windows? We may
never know! Happily,
the illustrated buildings
are still in existence
today. (Bryan Sales)

New Street, 1962. Many Ashfordians will remember Jack Scott's 'Bargain Shop' at no. 11 with the business of A. Sellers and Son butcher at no. 13 – one of the last butchers in the town to wear horizontal-striped aprons and still use sawdust on the floor prior to their closure in the 1980s. (Bryan Sales)

New Street junction with Gilbert Road, 1962. This splendid view illustrates the once-popular butchers at the junction of New Street and Gilbert Road. The corbelled cornerstone on the upper elevation of the building is repeated throughout the town and can be still seen at nos 39–41 Bank Street and at no. 83 High Street, for example. (Bryan Sales)

New Street, 1962. Although derelict here, upon closer inspection no. 16, the sign board above the door and the advert on the side wall of the premises indicates that C. Hayward & Son, whose main garage was further along New Street, uses this property for its cycle department. Back in the 1940s, seedsman Worger & Co. operated from no. 16 prior to moving to no. 75 High Street, where they remained until business ceased in the 1990s. (Bryan Sales)

New Street, 1962. Previously operated by Carlos and Thrale Ltd, the beer, wine and spirit retailers' premises at no 16a had been succeeded by Arthur Cooper in the same trade and his is certainly a name people will likely remember more readily. As these buildings were subject to an impending demolition application, Arthur Cooper moved his business to no. 2 Bank Street, from which it traded into the early 1980s. (Bryan Sales)

New Street, 1962. It's been at least 35 years since the memorable Hanson's fish shop and restaurant has been absent from Ashford, but respected owner John 'Hanson' Richardson, known for his local film making, and latterly his nephew Bill Saltmarsh, certainly left a lasting longing for their fantastic fish and chips. Even today, residents who frequented the popular eatery still speak of the excellent fish and chips served there. Previously home of Ball the brush maker, no. 15 was until recently home to furnisher Bakudi. (Bryan Sales)

New Street, 1962. When looking across the road from Hanson's, in 1963 your view would have been this trio of businesses at nos 18a, b and c, properties which for years until their demise had been in the same trade and in some cases the same family. From left to right; Andrews hairdresser, Ripley (Canterbury) Ltd dress agents and The Pets Shop. In 1982 and after surviving neighbouring demolition for the Ringway in the years prior, the trio of illustrated properties were demolished. Today realignment of Edinburgh Road passes through the site. (Bryan Sales)

New Street, 1962. Still a feature of the town today, these surviving properties at no 19 and nos 21–23 have been an array of different trades over the years, but notable longstanding tenants/owners have included T.K. Auto Panels at no. 19 and Peter S. Roberts insurance (latterly Swinton Insurance) at nos 21–23. At the time of this photo it was occupied by W.J. Humphrey's leather grindery and rubber boot factor and Frank Knock & Co., building contractor and undertaker (quite an unusual business combination that you perhaps wouldn't encounter today!). Hanson's can be seen creeping into view on the left. The former premises of Knock's survived mass demolition on the south side of New Street for the Ringway project. Its neighbours up to the recently demolished Prince Albert public house were all flattened in 1972. (Bryan Sales)

New Street, 1962. It's always great to see old advertising from the past, including this confectionery advert for Mackintosh (latterly Rowntree-Mackintosh) favourites alongside local auction posters. The location of this picture is alongside nos 21–23 New Street (Knock's premises). Incidentally, it's rather disconcerting to see a grave within the fenced area; one would hope that this is simply a display of Knock's workmanship, rather than the final resting place of some dearly departed family member, as it's not the most tranquil of locations today. (Bryan Sales)

New Street, 1962. As previously mentioned, there were a large number of properties and business premises sacrificed in the name of progress and this picture (indeed this whole chapter) illustrates some of them. Now part of the Ringway and a widened Forge Lane, nos 27–29 and 31, occupied at the time by E.C. Hudson, cycle agent, and Jan Adam, photographer, can be seen approximately ten years prior to their being buried forever. The black and white timbered premises of Knock's can still be picked out today, but the scene is very different with scores of cars passing through the area. (Bryan Sales)

New Street, 1962. Further along the south side of the street, residents will remember 'The Little Shop' at no. 83, adjacent to Earl and Co., second-hand car dealer, just out of view on the left. The 1960s must have been a busy time for sewer replacement, as we have seen earlier in the book. Many residential properties were also caught up in the redevelopment plans which involved compulsory purchase orders. (Bryan Sales)

New Street, 1962. This rather dramatic view illustrates that dereliction isn't a new thing, and that while this would be 'urban exploration' on a mini scale, many (including myself) would have loved to have a rummage (or 'rampage' as one acquaintance once put it) in an old shop/empty building such as this. The former premises of Dray & Son, boot and shoemaker, at no. 24 is reputed to have stood in this derelict state for some time. One can only pity the neighbours. The workshops of Haywards Garage can be seen on the left. (Bryan Sales)

New Street, 1962. These long-lost three-storey dwellings at nos 20–22, adjacent to the derelict premises of Dray & Son, actually appear to be occupied at this time. It's a wonder that the 1960s equivalent of a repairs notice wasn't served on the owner of no. 24, though in the world of planning enforcement, nothing surprises me anymore. The picture was taken 17 years after the Second World War ended, during which the substantial neighbouring hostelry The New Inn (at nos 26–30) was wrecked in a bombing raid in which Haywards Garage and nearby Snashall's Bakery took a direct hit, sadly resulting in loss of life. I wonder whether anyone recalls if the state of the building here was due to bomb damage? (Bryan Sales)

New Street, 1962. A piece of waste land (bottom right) marks the spot where the New Inn once stood. This splendid view also illustrates the filling station opposite Haywards main premises at nos 32–46 New Street. This large section of land had only become available as a result of the war, when several houses and businesses on this land were destroyed in a bombing raid. The premises of E.C. Wellman rag and metal merchants can be seen adjacent to the 'Go well – Go Shell' advertising board at no. 67a. It's a bit of novelty to see a pick-up belonging to a competitor garage parked outside Haywards' premises. (Bryan Sales)

New Street, 1962. On another occasion, the absence of parked cars gives an unobstructed view of the once-familiar business of Haywards, which was sold to Eastbourne motor group Caffyn's in 1967. The remainder of the illustrated buildings within the confines of the site were eventually demolished in 1972 and 1973 and for many years, the site was a council owned car park until Safeway opened on the site fronting Forge Lane and New Street in 1986. (Bryan Sales)

New Street, 1962. Another view of the across-the-road premises of Haywards Garage with Forge Lane pictured (far left) with the sign of scrap metal dealer C.J. Anderson's premises just visible between the buildings. This site was also used for the garage's used car department. Today the former Safeway premises dominates this corner and is now home to the Park Gym and a branch of the German discount supermarket Lidl. (Bryan Sales)

New Street, 1962. A fantastic view showing Haywards in a typical street setting of the 1960s, together with an array of old motor vehicles. Forge Lane and New Rents can be seen in the background (centre left). The tallest building of departmental store Lewis and Hyland's New Rents premises can be picked out just to the left of the Shell sign. (Bryan Sales)

New Street, 1962. A wonderful view illustrating the long-lost local landmark premises of C. Hayward & Son (Haywards Garage) at nos 32–46 taken from their filling station forecourt across the road. Haywards had to undertake a substantial amount of rebuilding on the site due to wartime bombing, as very few of their original buildings survived. Succeeded by Caffyn's, the prominent New Street site was sold for redevelopment in 1992. (Bryan Sales)

New Street, 1962. One of the firm's Lucas automotive lighting window displays in their post-war premises. This picture is taken at the junction of Forge Lane. (Bryan Sales)

New Street, 1962. The motorbike department of Haywards Garage. At the time of this picture, the business was specialising in Triumph and Ariel motorcycles. Ariel, which were founded in 1902, survived until 1967 when the manufacturer was taken over by BSA. (Bryan Sales)

New Street, 1962. Another splendid view illustrating the one-time premises of Haywards Garage looking back towards Castle Street. (Bryan Sales)

New Street, 1962. This view holds many fond sentiments for me as my mother used to take me into this shop when I was a young boy. A memorable view illustrating the long-forgotten premises of Violet Perkins' general stores at no. 50, adjacent to the premises of the Ozonic Mineral Water Co at no. 46. Violet ran her quaint and neatly stocked store until 1986, following the opening of the new Safeway store opposite. Caffyn's demolished Violet's old shop to make way for a bigger forecourt for their Austin Rover dealership, although the white-painted Ozonic premises disappeared some time before. (Bryan Sales)

New Street, 1962. The dwellings at neighbouring nos 52 and 54 were also demolished at the same time as Violet Perkins' shop. While it's no longer a public house, the former British Volunteer at nos 56–58 still survives today as self-contained flats, although the developer tried unsuccessfully to achieve full demolition of the historic inn. (Bryan Sales)

New Street, 1962. Two of the smart and well-kept dwellings at nos 91 and 93, which survived the enemy in the war years but were earmarked for demolition by planners. One can really imagine how devastated residents felt when their houses were as snatched from them. Generations of families had been born and brought up in these houses. Progress is quite often an awful thing. (Bryan Sales)

New Street, 1962. Those familiar with this part of town will remember some of the businesses that once graced the street in bygone times. This extremely rare view shows the premises of P.R. Stevens, tailor, at no. 95, a business premises that had obviously been converted from a residential house. (Bryan Sales)

New Street, 1962. Another rare and nostalgic view illustrating a New Street business that has almost faded from memory. The premises of J. Longley and Sons grocer and provision merchant is pictured at nos 97–99 New Street, just a stone's throw from the main High Street, but still many a housewife's choice when living in such a predominantly residential area. At this time, the store has Mace branding, which would have meant that the shop is owned, and a fee would have been paid for branding and marketing support to Mace who had only established itself in 1960, just two years prior to this photograph being taken. The Mace brand was founded in Ireland and continues to this day. (Bryan Sales)

New Street, 1962. Previously known as the premises of J. O'Keefe, dealer, some years previously, this picture illustrates an unidentified motorcycle parts dealer at no. 105 New Street that is not listed in any of the directories of the town. (Bryan Sales)

New Street, 1962. When the British Volunteer closed its doors as a public house in 2015, there was a fear locally that, as a victim of an increasingly unsustainable trade, it would end up like the Prince Albert on the opposite side of the road, which suffered an arson attack followed by years of dereliction. The former hostelry was then subsequently demolished. At one point, although not in any way derelict, there was a planning application put forward to demolish the Volunteer; however, after a local outcry, developers changed their minds and refurbished the building instead. Here we see the Volunteer in one of its many guises under Whitbread Mackeson ownership. (Bryan Sales)

New Street, 1962. The neighbouring dwellings of nos 60 and 62 New Street. Happily these still survive today. (Bryan Sales)

New Street, 1962.
Neighbouring properties nos 64 and 66 – some of the few remaining residences in the street. (Bryan Sales)

New Street, 1962.
An attentive mother watches over her child in the garden in this view of nos 70–72, which has an unusual curved entrance. The premises of Passmore, builders merchants, can be seen next door (left) at no. 74. (Bryan Sales)

New Street, 1962. A fantastic view showing no. 74 New Street during its time as Passmore, builders merchants. These premises will be remembered more for housing the longstanding business of respected TV and radio specialist David Easton, who moved to New Street from no. 51 Hempsted Street in 1972 following the compulsory purchase of his previous premises for the Tufton Shopping Centre. He had first established his business at Hempsted Street in 1960. Mr Easton retired in September 2018 and passed away at the beginning of 2019 after a short illness aged 81. He was faithfully served until his retirement by his assistant Kerry, who joined with the business in 1975. (Bryan Sales)

New Street, 1962. There were many more residential dwellings in New Street in previous times, with terraced houses stretching beyond the recently demolished Prince Albert (then known as the Prince Albert and Prince of Orange) on one side of the road and as far as what was until recently David Easton's premises at no. 74 on the other side. The terraced properties (right) with their unconventional dormers reached St Mary's School in this picture. This was a familiar sight for locals as well as those arriving into the town from the direction of Maidstone, but all was to change in 1973: the houses were demolished and the dangerous junction from Chart Road was removed when the new Ringway was built. One wonders what happened to the lovely old street sign at the junction (right). (Bryan Sales)

New Street, 1962. A sad reminder of some of the many residences that were lost to the hands of planners in the 1960s. These terraces at nos 76–114 had stood for hundreds of years and would be subject of preservation orders today. The junction of Magazine Road can be seen on the left with the Prince Albert and Prince of Orange public houses on the right at nos 111 and 109 respectively. Note the array of fantastic old adverts where there is an advert for 'The Cinema' advertising *Blue Hawaii* starring Elvis Presley. (Bryan Sales)

New Street, 1962. The unusual dormered properties at nos 113–141 New Street with Barrow Hill just creeping into view on the right. Note how narrow the road is here compared to today. (Bryan Sales)

New Street, 1962. Nos 113–141 pictured from the other direction, with the junction of Barrow Hill on the left. Many will remember the confectioner and tobacconist business of Mr C.J. Leaver further along the row of terraces at no. 127 (right). The auction notices affixed to the side of no. 113 advertise, on close inspection, poultry at Sheridan Poultry Farm Woodchurch, live and dead stock at Foxen Farm Charing Heath and Freehold Possession at Shepherdswell to name but a few. (Bryan Sales)

Magazine Road 1962. A rare and largely forgotten view showing nos 2–4 Magazine Road, together with the adjacent premises of E.K. Chittenden builder and contractor (joinery works), which was also the site of Beck and Martin, plumbers and decorators. Upon the construction of the Ringway, many of the feeder roads were altered considerably, including this one which went from a quaint T-junction to a seven-exit roundabout. The alteration necessitated the complete obliteration of the scene illustrated here. (Bryan Sales)

Hempsted Street, 1962. Once the home to scores of Ashfordians, this view illustrates long-lost Hempsted Street – a predominant residential area in the town's heart, which had a handful of businesses including two public houses. Through speaking with former residents, it seems to have been more a close-knit community than just any old street, and it's still recalled with an incredible level of affection. In master plans drawn up for the area in 1963 – the year after this picture was taken – Hempsted Street and its neighbouring streets were doomed, the area earmarked for what was initially known as the 'Hempsted Street Shopping Development' and eventually known as the Tufton Centre (latterly County Square). Hempsted Street was demolished between the 1960s and 1972 to make was for the scheme. The Invicta public house can be seen to the left. (Bryan Sales)

Hempsted Street, 1962. A lovely picture showing almost the full array of properties in the long-lost street as it heads towards New Rents and its adjoining streets of Middle Street, Regents Place and Tufton Street. (Bryan Sales)

Hempsted Street, 1962. These ancient terraces at the lower end of the street and which had survived two world wars, were some of the first properties to be demolished somewhat prematurely, only to become a council-owned car park. (Bryan Sales)

Hempsted Street junction with Middle Street, 1962. Many local residents will clearly remember these two imposing houses midway along Hempsted Street at nos 50–52, seen here in a largely derelict condition. (Bryan Sales)

Hempsted Street, 1962. The condition of the aforementioned properties at nos 50–52, is not any better from the rear. If anything, they look worse. (Bryan Sales)

Hempsted Street, 1962. The quaint old properties at the junction with Regents Place. It's sad to think that few fought for their preservation back at the time they were first at risk. Such historic gems are certainly worthy of fighting for. (Bryan Sales)

Hempsted Street, 1962. Some of the houses in the street, although quaint, lacked space, and one resident has built a lean-to extension. Back in such economically uncertain times, you were lucky to have the money to complete such a project. (Bryan Sales)

Hempsted Street, 1962. The rear access and gardens to some of the houses in the lower section of Hempsted Street. The tall building on the right is the Invicta public house. (Bryan Sales)

Regents Place junction with Hempsted Street and Tufton Street, 1962. A rare early morning view taken at the crossroads of Hempsted Street, Regents Place and Tufton Street, illustrating the two hostelries that many Ashfordians will remember: the Fremlin's-owned Coach & Horses (left) and the Wellington Hotel (right) also owned by the Kent brewery. The pre-midday mist obscures the buildings further down the road, but even so, the Elwick Club and the post office can be picked out (centre left) in the distance. Today, the shopping centre completely covers this site, making any chance to replicate the view totally impossible. (Bryan Sales)

Hempsted Street junction with Tufton Street and Regents Place, 1962. The presence of the looming mist creates quite a moody view looking towards the junction with the Wellington (centre left) and the Coach & Horses (centre right). This view was taken outside the former Wesleyan Chapel, which was used during this period by furnisher W.H. Gibbs as storage, and looks towards Godinton Road. (Bryan Sales)

Ashford Cattle Market, Elwick Road, 1969. A young lamb is held up for viewing as the auctioneer takes note of interest and bids from bystanders at the Elwick Road site. (Steve Salter Archive)

Ashford Cattle Market, Elwick Road, 1969. A fantastic view illustrating the livestock pens at Ashford Market shortly before substantial building alterations were made. The market company, which was established in 1856 at the Elwick Road site, is one of the oldest trading companies registered at Companies House. In subsequent years, the Elwick Road site was 'trimmed' somewhat by redevelopment and the High Speed 1 line, so in 1998, Ashford Market moved to a new site at Sevington near to the orbital road. The former market site stood empty for many years until a new cinema complex with restaurant units and a Travelodge opened on the site in 2019. (Steve Salter Archive)

Elwick Road junction with Bank Street and Godinton Road, 1964. A wonderful view showing the bustling street scene at one of the main arterial routes into the town centre. At this time, traffic flow in Bank Street appears to be two-way – something it hasn't been for decades. It is also to be noted that the streets and indeed its buildings look smart and clean compared to some of the buildings in the town today. The picture, taken from the roof of the former Corn Exchange, illustrates many businesses that have faded from memory, including sports outfitter Wright Brothers (centre left) at the corner of Bank Street and Elwick Road, a business that had disappeared by the 1980s. (Bank Street)

Middle Street, 1962. Still existing in part, this rare view illustrates Middle Street looking towards Hempsted Street with the former Methodist Church on the immediate left and further along on the left, the Kent Sweet Works and the premises of T. Headley the builder. On the right, Ashford Motors can be seen midway along on the right. Today, Middle Street is no longer a through road and serves predominantly as a service road and area for County Square Shopping Centre. (Bryan Sales)

Tufton Street junction with Bank Street, 1969. Until the redevelopment of Hempsted Street, there was a clear through route from Tufton Street into Hempsted Street then on to Godinton Road, Regents Place or New Rents. The route was stopped up permanently following the construction of the Tufton Shopping Centre that opened in 1975. The recently closed main post office (centre right) survived the redevelopment plans, but the neighbouring Elwick Club and almshouses were just two of the buildings demolished for the new shopping experience. Trice's florist and Kingsman bakery can be seen at the junction of Tufton Street on the left and right respectively. (Steve Salter Archive)

Tufton Street, 1969. Currently undergoing demolition to be replaced by residential dwellings, this rare view shows the premises of Farm and Garden (Lenfield) on the left at no. 23 with F.C. Wood funeral director next door at no. 21 and the Swan Hotel further along (centre left) at no. 15. Founded in Canterbury in 1850, Courts furniture store can be seen on the right, trading from the site of the old Ashford Picture Palace, which was demolished to make way for the new multi-floor showroom. This has since become a public house named The Phoenix following the furniture chain's collapse in 2004. Lenfield's premises at no. 23 has had many uses over the years, including a branch of Fads homecare and decorating specialist, a Nissan garage and a church for Ashford Christian Fellowship. The old police station and one-time Ashford Congregational Church can be seen further along on the right. (Steve Salter Archive)

Church Road, 1969. The much-missed purpose-built Ashford Library, which opened in 1966, can be seen here at the corner of Church Road and Norwood Street. Originally having a lecture theatre upstairs (which later became the reference library), the new facility was built on the site of houses that were bombed during the war. The town's previous library had been located in a timber building in Station Road. In 2010, a new Gateway Centre encompassing the library and other council services opened on the site following the demolition of the 1960s premises that had more than served its purpose. However, this was much to the chagrin of book lovers and those with an interest in local studies; the library had housed a local history collection to be proud of, but it was dispersed and many of the invaluable resources were taken to Maidstone, never to be seen again. This picture, taken early in this building's existence, shows the adjacent houses prior to their demolition for a library car park. (Steve Salter Archive)

Bank Street, 1961. A splendid view illustrating the wonderful array of shops, cafés and other businesses in Bank Street during the early 1960s, a time before town-centre traffic was largely banned. Ashford had a sense of completeness with the available variety of businesses back then, whereas today you often have to go elsewhere to another neighbouring town or out-of-town development to get what you need. This view looks towards the Upper High Street. (Bryan Sales)

Bank Street, 1961. This time Bank Street is seen from the junction of Tufton Street looking down towards Elwick Road and the market. It's quite odd to see traffic facing in the wrong direction with the traffic flow having been one-way in the direction of the High Street for many years. Much of the street's buildings and features have stayed relatively the same compared to other thoroughfares in the town centre, although the clear view through to the market seen here is rather dominated today by the new Elwick Place development. (Bryan Sales)

93

Bank Street, 1969. It's wonderful to see a bit of technicolour in this view illustrating the top of Bank Street where it meets the High Street with a splendid array of motor vehicles waiting at the traffic lights, a traffic accessory that hasn't been used in this part of town for some time. By the late 1960s and as illustrated, the traffic flow has changed to one-way as per today's regulations, but the area is heavily pedestrianised nowadays. Banning traffic and giving the street over to the pedestrian has its advantages, but deters passing trade and on-street parking, something that perhaps should never have happened. In many respects, pedestrianisation isn't all it's cracked up to be. (Bryan Sales)

Bank Street, 1969. This view (a personal favourite) illustrates everything the town was about in previous eras, and there is a wonderful atmosphere to be sensed from seeing how the town looked during a radically different period. Ashford was attractive and well-presented and indeed a desirable place to live and shop. On the left, the National Provincial Bank at no. 2a is certainly having a bit of an identity crisis with conflicting signage – one saying National Provincial Bank and another saying National Westminster Bank. To clarify, the two banks merged in 1968. Further along on the left, Kent-owned fruiterer and greengrocer Bodsham Farm Shops can be seen at no. 1a with Hepworth's gentlemen's outfitter at the corner of the two streets at no. 83 High Street. The longstanding premises of Lloyds Bank can be seen on the right. This bank was also the subject of various mergers and amalgamations, including the more recent guise of Lloyds TSB. (Steve Salter Archive)

High Street (Middle) and Kings Parade, 1969. This equally fascinating view taken just around the corner illustrates several once-familiar business names of the past. Take Kings Parade, for instance (right), with names like Granada Retail and Radio Rentals competing for trade alongside each other at nos 1 and 2 respectively. Further along the parade, Stuarts ladies' fashions can be seen at no. 2a, next door to Milletts Ltd clothiers and camping gear at no. 3. Advance Laundry Ltd operated from no. 4 at the time, with the Seeboard (South Eastern Electricity Board) showroom dealing in cookers, refrigerators and washing machines at the end of the parade at no. 5. Dixons the ironmonger can be seen in Middle Row (centre) at no. 7, and on the right of this view, many old Ashfordians still remember names such as Walter and Son shoes at no. 73 with Ruffle Brothers outfitters also at no. 73 and the revered business of Worger and Co., corn and seed merchants at no. 75, to name but a few. (Steve Salter Archive)

CHAPTER 5

....

SUBURBAN SNAPSHOT

Henwood, 1969. Built during the 1960s and completed shortly before this picture was taken, this rare view illustrates Henwood Industrial Estate not long after some of the first businesses had set up on the site. Today, names such as Kenhire, Lister-Wilder, WF Senate and even Kent Fire and Rescue call Henwood their home, but by 1970, only a handful of local business names had arrived at the industrial estate. These included: Rediffusion Limited, W.S. Profiling, Grimston, Houchin Ltd, Telemecanique Electrique, Burton Reproductions, Stewart Fraser and Unified Precision. Today the industrial hub is swamped by individual businesses with not an inch of green space to be seen. (Steve Salter Archive)

Henwood, 1969. Scores of residents of the 1950s and '60s will recall having the innovative Rediffusion TV and radio system at home and with many new-build houses, the company's cabling, which allowed TV and radio signals to be picked up through wired relay networks, was already installed as standard and identified by a single-dialled faceplate, often behind the television. It was the advent of cable satellite television that saw Rediffusion left behind, and by the late 1980s the company had been consumed by Granada. (Bryan Sales)

Hythe Road, Ashford, 1962. In all my years of studying Ashford's history, this is probably the rarest picture I've some across to date. This was particularly hard to identify initially but shows the long-lost houses at nos 11–25 Hythe Road, which once stood opposite East Hill Mill on the other side of the road where the river runs under the road. The old bridge, which was upgraded in the early 1970s, can be seen in the foreground. Today, Henwood Industrial Estate and Martyrs Field stand behind these houses. Just beyond the lamp post (right), where we can see monumental mason F.H. Russell's premises in the distance, marks the site where the entrance to Henwood stands today. (Bryan Sales)

Hythe Road, Ashford, 1962. A speeding motor car passes by no. 2 Hythe Road in this rare and largely forgotten view. The sign on the wall of the detached house which was demolished in 1971 indicates that the entrance to the one-time factory of Energen Foods can be accessed via Tufton Road. The demolition of the illustrated house made way for a new entrance as the Tufton Road entrance was no longer viable to use. (Bryan Sales)

Hythe Road, Ashford, 1962. An incredibly rare view illustrating the lower section of Hythe Road adjacent to the one-time business premises of monumental mason F.H. Russell, which stood on the immediate left at no. 27. It was to the rear of Russell's that heating and domestic engineering firm F. & J. Smith operated from. Although it appears that these residences were used for business too back in 1962, it is certainly not the case today. I am happy to report that the illustrated houses have survived the destruction experienced elsewhere in the town. (Bryan Sales)

Hythe Road, 1962. Now converted back into houses, this view illustrates nos 39, 41 and 43 Hythe Road during the era that no. 41 was L. Buller's general store advertising 'Eldorado' Supreme Ice-Cream, Nelson Tipped Cigarettes, Players Hearts of Oak tobacco and Brooke Bond Tea to name but a few. Next door, those with a musical talent and in particular an interest in piano, may remember going to see Mrs V. Henniker, teacher of Pianoforte at no. 43 for lessons. To look at these houses today, one would never imagine that they were ever used for business purposes. (Bryan Sales)

Hythe Road junction with Dering Road, 1962. Still trading from the same premises nearly 60 years later, this view illustrates the longstanding business of C.G. Earl, boot and shoe retailer and repairer, at nos 72–74 at the corner of Tufton Road and Hythe Road. In 2019, Earl's are one of the few remaining vintage independent businesses in the town, and their survival is something to be proud of. Note the regular use of advertising on the sides of buildings back then, something that the authorities largely disallow today. (Bryan Sales)

Hythe Road junction with Tufton Road, 1962. Not the most sensible of actions to leave your child's pushchair out in the road while you have a conversation. This view illustrates the business of J. Cook, grocer and general stores, at no. 76 Hythe Road, which has for many years been the home in recent times of Melvin Head Carpets. (Bryan Sales)

Hythe Road junction with Star Road, 1962. In recent times and for a number of years, nos 77 and 79 were home to Raj's Newsagent and general store, but here the familiar Hythe Road building at the corner of Star Road was the newsagents, confectioners and tobacconist business of D. & E.B. Dobson, which looks not that dissimilar to Arkwright's store in the BBC sitcom *Open All Hours*. Upon Raj taking ownership, the building was extended. (Bryan Sales)

Hythe Road, 1962. Still an instantly recognisable feature of Hythe Road today, here we can see the familiar parade of shops at nos 102, 104 and 106 when occupied by W.J. Thorn butcher, Hanson's fried fish restaurant and J.P. Stores, grocer. Only two of the three premises are used for business today; a fish and chip shop and a Chinese takeaway. (Bryan Sales)

Hythe Road, 1962. As nostalgic and lovely as they may be, this is a prime example of advertising gone mad and indeed not allowed today. One would hope that with such a sizable advertising board on the side of a private dwelling, the owners would have had some sort of recompense for their trouble. The allotments that once stood through the gate made way for the Gordon Close housing development a few years back. (Bryan Sales)

Hythe Road, 1969. Founded in 1630 as a free school by Sir Norton Knatchbull, the original school still stands in the churchyard of St Mary the Virgin, and the building known as the Dr Wilks Memorial Hall has housed the town's museum since 1989. The new grammar school illustrated opened on Monday 13 January 1958 and the movement of all the books and equipment from the old school took a whopping seven weeks! A reorganisation at the school had been confirmed at the grammar school in 1972 and, while keeping tradition with a number of the school's elements, it was renamed the Norton Knatchbull School in September 1973. In recent years, the school has undergone modernisation and refurbishment, and has also been progressively extended over the decades. (Bryan Sales)

Hythe Road, Willesborough junction with Albemarle Road, 1962. This picture illustrates the premises of G. Hughes and Co., grocers and newsagents, at no. 312 Hythe Road with Earl & Co., builders, next door at no. 314, in the days when independent grocers and newsagents were plentiful along the main arterial route into town. Today, substantially extended, the premises have in recent times been home to Ashford Security and the Earl & Co., funeral directors. (Bryan Sales)

Hythe Road, Willesborough (Mill Lane), 1967. The beautiful smock mill, built in 1869, was in a dilapidated and sorry state for many years following the industrialisation of milling in the 1950s, making mills such as this one largely redundant. Until 1989, the mill was used for storage and as a home, but in 1991, the mill was purchased by Ashford Borough Council and restored to its former glory. (Steve Salter Archive)

Hythe Road, Willesborough, 1962.
For many years, no. 398 Hythe Road (pictured) was the home of Dickinson's DIY, which was quite prominent in the 1970s in the days before the advent of many of the DIY chains that we are familiar with today. At the time of this picture, no. 398 was home to R. Farley, handicrafts. Today the familiar premises are home to Tiara & Tails bridal boutique. (Bryan Sales)

Lees Road, Willesborough, 1962.
An unobstructed view illustrating the 1950s semi-detached houses in neighbouring Hythe Road silhouetted beyond the trees. In the 1970s the land was developed for houses, and is today known as High Trees Close. The view taken from beneath the A20 Ashford bypass viaduct illustrates the original pre-war-constructed bridge which was demolished when the bypass was being converted to the M20 in 1978. (Bryan Sales)

Silver Hill Road, Willesborough, 1969. In the days before the rationalisation of ambulance services and the advent of services such as the South East Coast Ambulance Service, which provides such services in East Kent, each town had their individual ambulance stations, some of which were deemed too small and whose premises were sold on. The ambulance station in Silver Hill Road was one of these sites which was sold off for housing at the start of the millennium. Today it's Winslade Terrace – named after one-time Liberal Alliance candidate Fred Winslade. (Bryan Sales)

Hythe Road, Willesborough, 1962. The top section of Hythe Road looks absolutely deserted in this view illustrating some of the substantial trees, many of which have stood for hundreds of years. The area on the right was developed for housing, namely High Trees Close in the 1970s, and during the infamous hurricane of 1987 one of the massive trees fell through the roof of one of the houses. Thankfully, no injuries were reported. Further along to the left of the lamp post, Dunn's Hill House can be seen with its bay-window elevation. For many years the home of Wilfrid Geering, Dunn's Hill House was until recently Ashford Nursing Home, but closed due to substantial renovations and building works needed to bring it up to the required standards set out by the Care Quality Commission (CQC). (Bryan Sales)

Hythe Road, Willesborough, 1962. Planned and indeed commenced before the advent of the Second World War, the Ashford bypass opened between Maidstone Road, Ashford, near the Warren, and Hythe Road, Willesborough, in July 1957. The road scheme carved its way through the north of Ashford in a bid to reduce the gridlock in the town centre, although it could be argued that the gridlock then is nothing compared to today at peak times. This view illustrates the roundabout at the junction of Hythe Road and The Street. The house and many of its neighbours, including the farm of Little Lacton, disappeared in 1978/9 when work commenced on converting the bypass to junctions 9–11 of the M20. (Bryan Sales)

A20 Ashford bypass, Willesborough, 1962. Unlike the motorway with its hard shoulders for emergency use that supersedes the old bypass today, this layby, complete with its AA breakdown call box, was a familiar sight beside A roads up and down the county in the 1950s through to the 1970s, with the facility beginning to die out in the 1980s following the increasing popularity of mobile telephones. The Royal Automobile Club (RAC) also had similar boxes and it is reputed that each organisation's key fitted the other's call boxes. Willesborough Windmill and the neighbouring Willesborough Primary School can be seen in the background (right). (Bryan Sales)

A20 Ashford bypass, Willesborough, 1962. Another rare view illustrating the opposing carriageway and bridge over Lees Road and one of the houses in the distance, demolished when the bypass was converted into the M20. Note the lovely old road sign on the left on the picture. (Bryan Sales)

Hythe Road, Willesborough, 1965. A splendid view illustrating the beautiful Mediterranean-style house, Crooksfoot, with its green-tiled roof. It once stood on the site of Tesco Crooksfoot in Hythe Road near to junction 10. The house became derelict after the land adjacent was earmarked for the new M20 between Ashford and Folkestone, and its grounds were used temporarily as the site offices for the motorway between 1978 and 1981. It wasn't until 1991 that the almost completely derelict house was finally demolished. It stood approximately where the supermarket's filling station is now located. This picture illustrates the Hythe Road elevation. (Bryan Sales)

Hythe Road, Willesborough, 1965. This view illustrates Crooksfoot from what is now the car park of Tesco, showing the neatly cut lawns and well-stocked gardens. Many local people were mortified when the house became derelict and was finally demolished, including relatives of the previous owners. (Bryan Sales)

Willesborough Road, Kennington, 1969. Batchelors Foods had only been operating in the town for 12 years at the time of this picture. Their Willesborough Road site opened in 1957 together with its own railway sidings which were used prior to the roads being swamped by lorries as they are today. Despite several incidences of business uncertainty and numerous takeovers over the years, Batchelors is now part of Premier Foods and has ridden out many a recessional storm. Next door, Proprietary Perfumes Limited joined the neighbouring site in 1962 and after several name changes, still trades from the site today as Givaudan, a Swiss company that bought predecessor Quest International. Givaudan was founded in 1895. (Bryan Sales)

Bockhanger Square, Bybrook Road, Kennington, 1969. In the 1950s plans were passed to build on brownfield land in Kennington between Canterbury Road (A28) and Faversham Road (A251). Contracts were awarded in stages to different builders. Houses in the neighbouring private sector were built by T. Headley of Ashford and J.E. Webb of Eltham in London, whereas a large portion of the council housing was built by George Wimpey. A parade of shops and a takeaway, together with a community hall, were built within the scheme. These facilities opened in 1965 and over the years the hall was much used. In 2019, the owners of the hall, Ashford Borough Council deemed it 'unused' and in 'poor condition' and demolished it. It seems that the council's ultimate master plan is to build houses on the site, and they have rejected at the first hurdle a campaign to build a new hall. (Steve Salter Archive)

Belmont Road, Kennington, 1969. This early view of the estate illustrates the George Wimpey-built council maisonettes and three-bedroomed houses. Several of the council-owned properties here have since been purchased and are privately owned. The first of these blocks of maisonettes, nearest the junction of Bybrook Road and The Pasture, was named Heuel House and was opened by Herr Theodor Heuel – Burgermeister of Bad Münstereifel (Ashford's German twin town) on 3 August 1965. (Steve Salter Archive)

Bybrook Road, Kennington, 1969. A picture that holds many fond memories for me, this rare view illustrates Bybrook County Primary Infants School, which opened at Bybrook Road, Kennington, in 1963. The school's original name – Ashford Kennington South Junior Mixed and Infants School – was deemed too wordy, so original head, the late Donald Samuel, led an agreement to shorten the name to Bybrook C.P. Infants School. Following the construction of a new school to accommodate both age ranges, the former school, which was known as Phoenix Primary School by then, became derelict and was heavily vandalised. The former infants school was finally demolished to make way for an exclusive housing development in 2014, which I campaigned to have named Old School Mews. (Steve Salter Archive)

Faversham Road, Kennington, 1969. Nearly two years after it first opened, this splendid view shows the Towers Secondary School in Faversham Road, the brainchild and instant success of respected headmaster Geoffrey Foster. Mr Foster was given a blank canvas for setting up the school and, together with his faithful wife Jessie and first group of teaching staff, made the school something special with constantly high achievement in school league tables. Mr Foster was recognised for his services to education and was awarded the OBE upon his retirement in 1985. (Steve Salter Archive)

Canterbury Road, Kennington, 1969. In recent years the historic coaching inn along the A28, which was for many years known as the Golden Ball, was sold and extended, becoming the Old Mill. The popular public house and restaurant was completely different to the sleepy Shepherd Neame hostelry that was the Golden Ball. In its earlier guise, the pub was known for its bat and trap tournaments. (Steve Salter Archive)

Beaver Road, 1962. During the modernisation of Ashford station in the early 1960s and the removal of the traditional brick bridge and tunnels, a new bridge was built over the railway linking Station Road and Beaver Road. Further alterations in the 1990s saw the bridge rebuilt again with rumours that it needed to be further heightened due to an error, otherwise the international Eurostar trains wouldn't have been able to pass underneath it. (Steve Salter Archive)

Beaver Road, 1965.
Shops and businesses in many pictures of the past depicting the town of Ashford have quite often faded into oblivion as is the case here. This nostalgic view shows the long-lost business of C.J. Kennett, tobacconist and newsagent at no. 16, and County Motors tyres, batteries, etc., at no. 14a. This whole row of properties and businesses, including the neighbouring Butchers Hotel and Victoria public house, were demolished prematurely in 1999 leaving much of the site derelict until quite recently. (Bryan Sales)

Beaver Road, 1965.
An extremely rare view illustrating the presence of County Motors, which once operated on the west side of Beaver Road between The Cinema at the corner of Newtown Road and Trumpet Bridge (pictured). In this view, the former stationmaster's house can be seen between the two buildings in the background. Following the takeover of the building on the right by automotive business John Wilment, the 'Used Car Dept', seen here, was redeveloped and larger premises were built. Following the departure of John Wilment in the early 1970s, DIY chain B&Q opened a new store in the former garage premises in 1972. The store was opened by TV personality Derek Nimmo. (Bryan Sales)

Beaver Road, 1968. This view illustrates the old Trumpet Bridge before road alterations took place to strengthen the ancient crossing over the river. Ashford swimming baths are further along on the right. This lower section of Beaver Road beyond the bridge was notorious for flooding in bygone eras. (Steve Salter Archive)

Beaver Road, 1965. This view and the next give a sentimental insight into two of the long-lost businesses in suburban Ashford from an extremely different decade. Many of the individual shops in this parade in Beaver Road have since been converted into flats, and this may well be one of them. A wonderful image showing the premises of G.M. Smith, tobacconist and confectioner, at no. 53, with a sub-branch of Lloyds Bank to the right at no. 55a and the neighbouring business of F.G. Bell, wool and fancy goods at no. 51. (Bryan Sales)

Beaver Road, 1965. Further along the parade, other businesses trading here at this time included (from left to right) Co-operative Society laundry and cleaners at no 57, Ealham's newsagent and tobacconist at no. 59 and A.P. Hartman's chemist at no. 61. None of these businesses are still trading today. (Bryan Sales)

Beaver Road. 1965. Better known in recent years as Chinese takeaway Hong Kong Kitchen, this splendid view illustrates the grocer's business of W.L. Owen at nos 232–234 Beaver Road. The takeaway business, one of the oldest in the town, has only recently changed its name to Beijing House. (Bryan Sales)

Beaver Road, 1965. On the opposite side of the road, and still a chemist's premises in 2019, here we can see the business of pharmacist L.A.H. Marks. For many years, residents will have become more familiar with the current Ashworth's Chemist at no. 229, with owner and pharmacist Mr C.M. Shah. (Bryan Sales)

Wotton Road, 1969. Not well known nowadays, but many of us from a wide age range will have used the rub-off lettering of Letraset at some period in their life. Letraset were one of the first major names to set up a commercial base in Ashford in the 1960s. In 2012 the business was acquired by French company the ColArt Group who made the decision to close the longstanding Ashford site the following year. The former Letraset building is now leased out to companies for multiple storage solutions. (Bryan Sales)

Beaver Lane, 1969. Built in similar style to its sister Sydenham House surgery at the old site in Church Road, Ashford, this view illustrates the old Brookfield Surgery during the days of Dr Montgomery, Dr Bayley, Dr Jonas, Dr White and Dr Dhillon, to name but a few. At the time of writing, the surgery, which is still part of the Sydenham House Group (whose main base is at Mill Court), is operated from the former surgery premises of Dr Kazmi and called Musgrove Park Medical Centre. Popular and respected GP Dr Menon runs most of his weekly surgeries here nowadays. (Bryan Sales)

Stanhope Square, 1969. All seems quiet in this rare view illustrating Stanhope Square in South Ashford. Back in the 1970s and '80s, the estate was notorious for trouble, and it was a no-go area if you didn't have your wits about you. In recent years though, the estate, reputed to have been built on a prisoner of war camp of the same name, has been transformed in many respects. The high-rise 1960s maisonettes are no more, and the estate has tidied up its act. Credit for this is largely due to respected councillor Palma Laughton, who has tirelessly fought for better fortunes for Stanhope – the estate on which she lived. Her determination and spirit certainly paid off. The illustrated square was redeveloped as part of the plans. (Steve Salter Archive)

ACKNOWLEDGEMENTS

Over the years many local people and companies have been extremely kind and patient in assisting me with my research. Many have given me very valuable information, which has enabled me to put together an interesting record of the history of Ashford and to build up a substantial photographic collection.

I have been overwhelmed by the continued support for, and enormous success of the resulting published works: *Changing Ashford*, *Ashford Then and Now*, *Ashford 1950–1980*, *Around Ashford*, *Remembering Ashford*, *Ashford Then and Now Revisited*, *Ashford in the 1960s and '70s*, *Ashford – A Rare Insight* and *Ashford – Visual Recollections*. I am also very grateful to those who have followed my fortunes over the past 35 years. Without their kindness, this new book wouldn't have been possible. As ever, I have received much generosity from several individuals and organisations that have readily allowed me to use their pictures. I would therefore like to give heartfelt thanks to the following:

James Adams; the late Richard Filmer; Sue Cowan; Edwin Bartlett; Vasoulla and David Sims; Sylvia and Sid Marsh; Neville Marsh; the late Peter Goodwin; Mrs Pam Goodwin; David Worsley; Geoff Mathews; Sam Mathews; Jim Ashby and Mrs Joan Ashby; Howard and Christine Green; June Wenborn at Ashford Gateway Plus (Library); Daniel Wright, Robert Barman, Mandy Curtin and all at the Kent Messenger Group; Pam Herrapath at Ashford Borough Council; Alastair Irvine; Roger Lindfield; Bryan Badham; Allen and Mrs Christine Wells; Palma and Frankie Laughton; Jo-an Baxter; Mary O'Neill, Christine Baker; Bob and Daphne Davidson; Dukelease Properties; Owen Holmes; the late David Easton; Lindsay White; Richard Stafford; John Kennedy, architect; Terry and Eunice Burch; Katherine Burch; Nigel Gould; Karin Crittenden; Lee Blackman; Jessie Foster; Edith Neilson; Steve Godden; Steve Rabson; Les Freathy; David and Jean Emmett; Susan Jordan; Neil Jordan; Paul Jordan; Martin Symonds; Matt Symonds; Dave and Jean Read; Julia Easton; Lesley Easton; Christopher Easton; Paul Kennedy.

Since May 2017, following the untimely death of my friend Richard Filmer – a respected and acknowledged authority on the history of Ashford – I have been the proud and humbled owner of Richard's complete Ashford picture and ephemera archive, but not only this: also his wider tools and trades collection, as well as his hop-picking picture archive. He was something of an expert in all these fields and it is important to me that in honour of Richard's memory, his name is still acknowledged for the tireless work he undertook in charting the changes in local and trade history.

I would finally like to express a special thanks to my special friend James for taking me under his wing and looking after me through challenging times with my mum, who has vascular dementia.

Thanks are also due to anyone whose name has not been acknowledged here, either through an oversight or because the original source or present ownership of pictures is unknown or unavailable.

Finally, many thanks to Matt Falcus at Destinworld Publishing for having faith in me, and to my long-standing and fantastic editor Michelle Tilling; I am very grateful to you both for helping me to produce yet another successful book.